I0144951

The Diary Of A Warless Warrior

02/06/10 - 08/11/10

A Book Of The Blog
www.1nomad.blogspot.com

by Mike Jones

The Diary Of A Warless Warrior

The following is dedicated to my long suffering family and friend.
A recent addition to those I'd like to thank, have been my long johns. Thank you for your precious warmth, and thank you T.K Maxx for only charging me a tenner for them I understand now why a mans age was counted in the number of winters he'd survived... Thank you Reader, please do enjoy...

Wednesday 02/06/10

A famous Diarist by the name Pepys once wrote "a day unrecorded is a day wasted". I do agree to an extent, but I also think he was pretty biased towards his fact recording hobby. If it wasn't for Pliny the erm..Younger? Elder? one of them anyhow, the eruption of Pompeii would remain that much more mysterious.

I have resolved henceforth to record my days activities. For posterity, for wealth (I think not), for fun, we'll see.

I am a 24 year old, currently employed with a partner and child. There are a fair few of us out there, thankfully, not all like me.

So. This morning, I overslept. Despite only being ten minutes after the time I should've arrived, I took a day for the Queen, otherwise known as a duvet day... although there wasn't much duvet today. Took Emma, my partner, to work, then went about researching the recipe for nettle beer, and proceeded to pick 100 nettle tops. Why? Because I'm currently reading The Tree House Diaries by Nick Weston and have taken it upon myself to test the recipes he describes.

Nettle beer

- 100 nettle tops (with leaves 4-6)
- 12 litres (2 ½ gallons) water
- 1 ½ kg (3lb) sugar
- 50g cream of tartar
- 15g brewers or beer yeast

After my foraging I returned home to realise I was without Cream of Tartar. The whole 50g of it that was required. So off I went to town. The problem is I'm a great believer when it comes to burning my black gold aka fuel/oil in always getting more than one job done, so soon I had a long list. Chuck in some impulse buys like a wind up torch/charger, sixteen AAA batteries, a large stock pot, and by god you've just spent nigh on eighty pounds!

To make myself feel better for the expenses and todays loss of earnings, I've listed my 'as new' SAT Nav on eBay. Lets hope it does well!

The Diary Of A Warless Warrior

My mate Luke popped up to kill time and help me scout a good camp site for this weekend. In the end we collected the women and made an evening of it by ordering pizza. The highlight also being my opportunistic shooting of a jackdaw perching on our aerial, sadly I only winged it. Before I could despatch it as quickly and humanely as possible, Bill, the next door neighbours cat nicked it and finished it off somewhere in the bushes. Bugger me did the rooks and other jackdaws go NUTS! Was like a scene from 'The Birds'.

Knackered now, best not lose any more of next months pay check!

Thursday 03/06/10

Actually made it into work today, and quickly wished I hadn't. Recently management had a cost cutting brainwave, take vehicles off the road, make the staff work longer and harder. All under the guise of cutting fuel usage and CO_2 emissions.

I work on recycling collection. You'd be forgiven for thinking we used electric-hybrid trucks, or at least bio-diesel. No. These clapped out trucks are nearly 10 years old and 'hand me downs' from other contracts. They do 8 miles to the gallon and still management are happy to send such a gas guzzler 10 miles or more to collect ONE box because one lazy bastard didn't put it out early enough and had the gall to complain to the council. Rather than say "tough titties" Veolia (the recycling contractor) will still send a massive kerbsider for it as a missed box incurs a £40 penalty, so they say...

We get paid for ten hours regardless of whether we finish after 6 or 8 hours and then go home. But they have understandably decided to get their moneys worth by increasing the size of the rounds to 1200 plus properties. So in sweltering conditions, we loaded 8 tonnes of crap bound for china for 10 hours 6am - 4:30pm.
Got home with a strained back muscle, a sunburnt neck and face as well as severe dehydration...
Had a bath then tea, now its bedtime. oh and had to pick Emma's dad up, bring him over, then run him back. I'm shagged out, and now raring to do it all again.

Just living the dream...

4

Friday 04/06/10

Just another day at the Office...

Got up as required, got carried away checking the bank balance and was late leaving by 15 minutes.

Was hardly worth rushing as we only got pissed around anyway. I hate work. Its not because I'm work shy, I assure you. Employment is ridiculous and unnatural.

Think about it. Instead of spending the day doing things essential to our living and survival, we spend at least 8 hours a day, 5 days a week doing the same task over and over. So rather than doing many varied tasks and activities, we sell our souls and time for gold to pay someone else for something you could have made/done yourself and perpetuate the cycle.

Is it any wonder depression is so common? Unfortunately if everyone had my desire to not earn and rather, work to live, the Government would have a severe income problem!

Wanted to sod off and go camping, but had loads of cleaning and washing up to do. Didn't finish the chores til gone 7pm. Settled for making a fire in the garden, and falling asleep by it. Got pretty cold so jacked it in.

Off to Wales tomorrow to visit the Lammas Project. An Eco village/ Smallholding jobby. Should be interesting, might get to go camping in time for the weather to turn shit....

Will let ya know.

Saturday 05/06/10 - Wednesday 09/06/10

WOW!

What an adventure! Went to Lammas as planned, had a great day. Left, car broke down! Retreated to a petrol station we'd passed (car would start, appear to be fine, then die) and filled up in case of dodgy fuel, then tried again. Same thing at exactly the same place which happened to be the sign reading "Welcome to Carmarthenshire". Check engine light would flash then engine would lose power and die. Decided to return to Lammas as a point of reference for the RAC, plus we wouldn't be on our own.

Ended up staying with a fantastic family for the best part of three days and have now decided to live there with them!

I cannot describe the feeling we've been left with. A calling. My soul has awakened. My energy is channelled. At Lammas we'll be growing our food and building a house...first steps are to fix car, sell/swap for camper/caravan. Sell our crap. Easy!

Just have to slug out our jobs for another month or two.

Now I have the system by the balls and not the other way around.

The Diary Of A Warless Warrior

Paul W running us through his build and explaining the planning battle

The Mill Pond

The Diary Of A Warless Warrior

Nigel and Cassies reciprocal roof.

View across the valley from Simon D's plot

The Diary Of A Warless Warrior

Morning at Lammas, Tir-Y-Gafel

Mill pond in the morning at Lammas, Tir-Y-Gafel

The Diary Of A Warless Warrior

A peek inside Simon D and Jasmine's House

The Slug Refuge...

Thursday 10/06/10

Went to work. Bloody tough day. Also finding it really hard to keep focussed. I JUST WANT TO QUIT AND GET ON WITH THINGS!!!!!

Spoke to my parents who seem really quite supportive, which I definitely did not expect. They advised us to buy a caravan rather than a camper van. Bid on one on eBay that evening for £200 with awning. Will probably lose it to someone with deeper pockets.

Emma's Mum is now on board and she says her Nan is willing to help financially. I have a fair few concerns. Lots of thoughts flying around right now, doubt I'll sleep well.

NOT looking forward to being pissed about at work tomorrow. Hate my job now. Stops me doing what I need to do to get on with my life.

Home - For the foreseeable future...

Tuesday 15/06/10

Boy am I pooped! Been a hectic few days. Am doing my best not to let days go past unrecorded but it seems I need to be a bit more disciplined.

Handed my notice in Friday, with no intention of serving the one week required. I did warn the boss I would contract a "mysterious and intense" 4 day long illness that might dent my attendance record. The message obviously wasn't communicated judging by the phone call today from my rather annoyed supervisor. I did consider going in but soon thought better of it when I realised my core motive for doing so would be money. NO. I refuse to sell out to the system.
When I handed my notice in I'd calculated that the days I'd worked plus the holiday accrued was enough to fund my direct debits which I shall soon be cancelling.

To have gone in and suffered because of greed for gold would have been negating the point of this entire exercise.

That said, I am prepared that should the shit hit the fan and the money raised from the sale of our belongings not be enough, I would work a short

The Diary Of A Warless Warrior

period. But that scenario is exceedingly unlikely if we stick to the plan...

Saturday was supposed to be spent preparing for the car boot sale Sunday. Instead we bought a caravan I'd seen with a FOR SALE sign and £200 pegged to a curtain. The owner randomly, and very kindly lowered the price to £150 and we were in for one hell of a bargain!

4 berth, good condition, WITH awning and poles!

Turns out it was her late fathers, but get this, when I mentioned to her brother I was after a 4x4 he gestured over his shoulder to a rough and ready looking Land Rover Discovery! He initially said he wanted £800/£750 for it but admitted it needed a new water pump. I text later on the Monday and lied I'd only been offered £500 for my car so could he meet me at £600, he agreed!

Got £600 for my Galant on eBay and better still, found a water pump for a Discovery for £15! The gods appear to be on my side (at present)

Now whilst the sale of my car has gone pretty smoothly so far (being paid for and picked up Friday I hope) Emma's car has been a different story... hopefully it'll sell for £250 a snip considering we paid £750 barely a year ago for it!

The car boot sale went okay I suppose. Overslept which didn't help but got rid of perhaps half the stuff we took and made £32 profit, promptly swallowed at the petrol pump along with £19 more of my meaningless currency. Took all the unsold stuff to the charity shop....

Anyhoo. Solar panels arrived today from Maplin god bless em. £199.99 60watts. Just need a proper battery for it Also need to work out how the electrics go together in the caravan. I have a hunch I know where the switch is...

Wednesday 16/06/10

Bit of a rough day. Only due to a tiff with Emma. Started out ok, dropped Frances, my daughter, at school, Emma at work.

Came back, had a shave with my new cut throat razor. Only the 2nd time I've used it and not a nick yet! Then a soak in the tub. By the time I'd cleaned out my ears it was getting on for 10/10:30. Hopped out, packaged up some PC games I'd sold then off to the Post Office and over to my parents to return their laptop from being fixed by Emma's colleague. Also took over a digital photo frame about 6 months after I bought it for them. God I'm crap sometimes.

Had a bite and a chat then off to pick Emma up so she could grab some lunch at home.

I was then overwhelmed with siesta syndrome and succumbed by napping on the sofa whilst Em had a sarnie. Must've given the impression that's all I currently do all day!

Tiff started over glass and plastic. I know. Out of context its ridiculous, even in context its stupid. Emma said we could keep our water in glass demi johns whereas my idea was to use one of my plastic brewing barrels with a tap and is 5 times the size. My argument was based on weight, hers on something her mother had said about plastic leeching chemicals. I was also talking broadly due to the legal restrictions on towing and 'train weight'.

Anyhoo. Without a word of thanks from Emma for our midday rendezvous and taxiing, I decided she could walk home. Weather was fantastic plus it'd free me up to actually get something useful done.

After picking up Frances from school I finally got round to sorting through and emptying my wardrobe. 4 bin bags worth! Might try and sell at a car boot sale this weekend but they're most likely headed for the charity shop.

Luke came up for a chat and to chill. Always a pleasure.
Can't wait to do something else tomorrow that can summon my dream forward into reality. Even if it is just by one small step.

Thursday 17/06/10

Not much to report today really. Did the usual taxiing then came home and watched 'Slumming it' with Kevin McCloud. Interesting stuff.

Intended to clean the car inside and out at my parents. Decided to do it tomorrow as Uncle Ken arrived two minutes after we did (Fran & I).

Watched France vs Mexico world cup game - Wanted Mexico to win. Have always liked them after watching I think the '94 world cup when Campos played for them. He was so entertaining. A striker who could also go in goal. He was a brilliant little guy... Anyhoo they won 2:0 (Mexico)

Friday (At Last) 18/06/10

A sale. A purchase.

After attending my daughters "work of the week" assembly. I took the opportunity to call on our friends Andy and Bridget, with an ulterior motive... Aside from a hot brew, I desired the use of a pressure washer and a hoover. They kindly obliged and I cleaned my Mitsubishi Galant inside and out in preparation for the eBayer who would be purchasing it.

Really nice chap came, seemed pretty genuine, paid the agreed £600 in cash & left.

I then took that cash and bought the Land Rover Discovery an hour later. Need to get the water pump replaced but will attempt that myself if the part arrives in the post. Should save me £50-£100!

All in all a pretty good day.

Lets see what tomorrow brings.

Saturday 19/06/10

Landy water pump came. Of course I was in the bath, and yes on my own as Emma and Fran had nipped out to the shops. Bloody typical.

My Dad came over with some anti freeze and coolant and to look at the engine and advised me not to bother doing it myself...

Kinda followed his advice. I took it to a mate. Unfortunately, and as I suspected. It wasn't the water pump. We drained, flushed, and refilled the coolant system, but still something was wrong. The landy didn't overheat, but the coolant was overflowing and becoming pressurized over the prescribed 15 psi.

A neighbour quickly diagnosed the problem. I've been sold a land rover with a blown head gasket. Bummer.

Anyhoo. Being as I got it so cheap (and its now clear why) I can afford to get it repaired. Gunna do some serious bargaining come Monday. My dad is picking us up tomorrow for a roast dinner. Yum Yum.

Tuesday 22/06/10

Disco Stu, for that is his name, is very poorly. So poorly in fact, I've replaced him. Instead, with the kind help of the mother in law, we have a Vauxhall Monterey aka Isuzu Trooper.

Disco Stu had a Pre-MOT which he passed, however, he has indeed blown a head gasket. The cylinder head has been sent off to be inspected for cracks. Poor Stu.

The Monterey had a most interesting owner. An 80 year old gentleman, who certainly knew his stuff, and whose business was selling law books on eBay. His wife loved our daughter and whilst the women chatted, I was led to the bottom of his house to a porta cabin wherein was stored an extraordinary record of British legal heritage. Handwritten and bound in leather, were many many volumes recounting writs of the king as far back as 1475! He had in fact purchased the collection from Earl Spencer, Princess Diana's brother, keen to flog the families treasures, apparently to "Live it up with some crumpet in Wales..." . Interesting.

Wednesday 23/06/10

Right I'm tired. Not done much though. My dad picked up Emma and Fran in the morning which left me free, and bored, having to stay housebound to wait for some estate agent to inspect the house. The very same agent who didn't bother to turn up. So now I have another day of lonely idleness to look forward to.

Disco Stu's cylinder head was warped! Had obviously been allowed to overheat in the past to such an extent that not only did the temperature deform solid metal but also melted a sensor and knackered the heat plugs. Still, I've been assured the whole lot will amount to no more than £400 so have relisted him on eBay at £1294. I hope I can make another £300 as I did on the Galant but if someone offers a grand I'll cut my losses and take it.

Watched England scrape a 1-0 victory against Slovenia. Bad news as it means we face ze Germans this Sunday. We're buggered in my opinion.

Watched a program called 'Erasing David' all about the information collected on us by corporations and the government. Scary shit man. He was a pillock though. He went 'on the run' from two private eyes he'd hired to track him down. His aim was to last 30 days... he lasted 18 after his wife called him and made him attend a baby scan which the P.I's knew about through some sneaky tactics. Typical. Brought down by a moody woman. So many great men have fallen that way. If the Creationists are to be believed the first was Adam... Samson's up there too, along with Greek and Roman heroes. Poor Bastards.

Thursday 24/06/10

Feels as though the dream is fading. Getting bogged down by the grinding routine of this 'modern' living. Alot of my thinking time today has been devoted to how I can also disappear from the radar. To the extent of wearing sunglasses and a balaclava in and around towns and cities. Bit of a paradox considering that by hiding your identity you then become more visible. Granted, no one knows who you are, but conversely, I doubt it would take long before Big Brother would want to find out... Muslim women get away with it, hmmm there's an idea...naaahh....

Our man in Wales called to cancel this weekends visit. Pretty huge blow as I was relying on it to regain focus and perspective. A reminder of what is waiting at the other end... Just have to try and find a way to use the weekend to do something constructive. Something to bring the dream that one step closer. The trouble is, with the way my tired mind and body is, all I want to do is wallow in this misery.

Nice weather today though....

Sunday 27/06/10

Friday was busy-ish, got the tracking and wheel alignment done on the new 4x4. Just as well too as we decided that we would go ahead and venture off to Wales in search of Tipi Valley.

We packed the necessary equipment in case we didn't find it as it is notoriously off the beaten track.

We got most of the way there before my phone battery died and I just drove on, navigating with a combination of instinct and Google maps memory.

We found a spot that felt bloody close to Tipi Valley and at around 22:00 pitched a tent and bedded down.

I awoke around 5am Saturday morning and had a scout around. All the signs were there. A row of vans and converted campers, cars with maps chargers etc, evidence of traditional crafts and woodworking.

Found some wood and got a fire going, for breakfast we had rice...quite a good porridge equivalent!

Filled our water bottles at an eerily deserted farmhouse save for the cat who had met us the previous night and guided us to our camping spot. Transpired the occupants were at Glastonbury!

By following the track we then knocked on the last farmhouse on the track where the owner informed us we were in the right place, here was the fabled Tipi valley!

Back to the car to gather our stuff and off to the 'Big Lodge'.

The Diary Of A Warless Warrior

We were greeted by Henry, a young chap with dreadlocks who put on a brew and answered our endless stream of questions and listened to our story. He introduced us to Lola and her three children. She in turn invited us to join the whole (or rather the remainder) of the community who were off to the village fair. On the walk down we picked a 12 foot bramble for the competition of who could find the longest bramble...

I joined the Valley men in a football tournament and seriously paid the price. Ouch! Cramp set in quickly due to the heat.

After Carol the Drunk was evicted we had the Big Lodge to ourselves for the duration of our stay.

Another 5am start for me on the Sunday. For me, in this lifestyle, it seems right to start the day when the sunrises, and turn in when it sets.

Frances got to ride two of the three horses with Jaz, I'll probably be heading down to the Yurt of my team mate and fellow brewing enthusiast, Dan, to sample some of his much lauded Elderflower wine.

Another hot day so should be most refreshing, undecided as to whether we'll go back home this evening...

Wednesday 30/06/10

Stayed Monday and headed home

Stopped off at the services for a burger and coffee, a good slap of what we want to leave!

Forced back into the services a couple of junctions later, as the food left me battling my eyelids. Not only did I have a snooze, but so did Em and Fran. Sadly all we've done that's positive is head over to the caravan on Tuesday to stock it with dried stuff. Em & Fran were off work and school until the doctor could rule out this e-coli. Emma's Mum managed to pick it up on holiday with Fran . Means our forced march to Farnborough could be cancelled due to Emma's sister Nicola being paranoid of infection.

Hope her paranoia lasts as I can't be arsed.

Otherwise it's back to the drudgery of mainstream life...BORING. Am tired but I think not from exercise but just wanting the day to end. Would probably feel better if I were sleeping in the garden. Going to read my Primitive Living book as bedtime research.

Wednesday 21/07/10

Am pretty annoyed with myself for not being more disciplined and writing more often. My excuse should be I've been really busy, but this just isn't true. The busyness has been more sporadic.

There was the whole moving and ruthless shedding of worthless junk, including some important stuff, like my land rovers v5 registration document

Have now sold that damn discovery for £800, so lost £200. Buyer insisted on having it MOT'd. Cheeky bastard did his best to get me to pay for it too!

Today was Frances' last at her current school, which now frees her up, finally.

Thursday 22/07/10

Had a pretty relaxed day, bar the afternoon.

Morning was spent in blissful distraction finding little unimportant things to do in order to avoid the washing up.

Took Emma along with Fran to her friend Jaynes in South Cerney. Watched ALOT of TV...Packing it in while I still can!

On the way back I dropped off Em & Fran in town, and had to nip back and collect the money for the Land Rover. After handing pretty much all of it over to Emma for my share of the Monterey, I paid the rest into my heavily overdrawn account.

Luckily we ate cheaply that night having been invited for a meal down at my parents neighbours.

Whilst down there Fran, and subsequently Anne, Em and David ended up playing all sorts of instruments ranging from the recorder, piccolo, clarinet, tenor and some rather wonderful stringed instrument whose name escapes me.
Looked rather like a foot.....

All in all a good day.

Friday 23/07/10

Made the decision to try and spend the day in a constructive fashion. So it started with the washing up and ended with a trip to Attwoolls...

Bought £160 of mostly useful and essential stuff i.e. new 110ah leisure battery, wellies, compass, rain suit for Fran. Plus some eccentric things like an Aussie leather bush hat - sexy!

The latter part of the day was filled with a visit from my buddy Luke and piss arsing about with my air rifle which lead to discovering the culprit behind its recent inaccuracy - a wobbly barrel. Unfortunately being a cheapy £50 job a fair few years ago, the offending part was sealed and unable to be adjusted. Guess what I'm doing tomorrow...

My new Edgar brothers MOD 60 .177 Air rifle vs my old Beeman

Saturday 24/07/10

Got my new rifle! Wow is it a beast. Spent the day zeroing and letting it all settle in. Parked in Asda car park in Gloucester, so whilst I went to pick it up, Em & Fran went for a mooch and resupply. Joined them inside and went for a coffee and a cake.

We've been cramming in the modern conveniences recently such as McDonalds, KFC, and loads of TV and computer! 20:30 went out with the air rifle to see if I couldn't bag a pigeon in the church yard over the road. Turns out I couldn't. Wasn't disappointed though. I love wandering the fields as quietly as possible. In hunter mode, your eyes are everywhere, so for once, you notice all that's around you. You hear the different bird calls, notice the bats darting over your head. Am very eager to do more of that and am very excited to think of all the countryside that will be at my disposal in this new life of ours.

Sunday 25/07/10

After a lazy morning, went to Emma's mums for Sunday lunch. Stuffed myself and promptly curled up on the sofa for a snooze. Didn't last long...ended up watching Oliver Twist with Fran. Feeling pretty crap after catching one of those deadly strains of cold. The type that would fell all but the hardiest of individuals. Lucky I'm such a hero!

I maintain its Emma's fault. I'm a hot sleeper that wears the minimum in bed and normally starts the night with the bedding half on and half off. Now SHE insists I sleep to her right and because of the end of the bed she's chosen, this means I must sleep by the window. 1) This is most incredibly inconvenient. It means I have to clamber over her in the morning as I am normally the first up and 2) it means the cold air from the window is funnelled onto me through out the night. Due to my state of undress, this has resulted in a fatal cold.

Things are gunna change around here...!

Monday 26/07/10

Still suffering...At deaths door I think... Still like the hero I am I soldier on. Albeit with a little three hour nap at midday.

Another run to town and a quick trip to our friends to say goodbye. Last night Fran and I stayed up late watching the Simpsons online. Em was out drinking, the dirty stop out. To take the mick, she came home around 22:30, drummed me out of Frans bed and then watched me make and assemble ours. (Have to pack away each morning to enable us to have a sit down area. A big downside to living in a caravan!)

Moving day tomorrow! yey!

23

Tuesday 27/07/10

Alarm was set for 04:30. Optimistic I Know. Eventually stirred at 05:00. As predicted we overran my departure time of 06:00, instead leaving at 07:30. Inevitable when there are females in tow... and she still forgot the porridge

The journey down was slow but passed quickly. Punctuated by only one stop at the services for breakfast and a well deserved coffee. I hammered on and on to Emma about weight in the caravan when we moved in and the tyres told me how much she'd listened when I hitched the van up...women...

Arrived around 11:45 and pretty much hit the ground running. First off was the positioning of the van. Then I got it stable. But stable just is not good enough. IT MUST BE LEVEL!... on a f***ing wonky diagonal hill. Cheers.

Much strained jacking eventually led onto erecting the awning where I amused myself with innuendos aplenty. Poles, rods, shafts, holes, positions, tightness etc etc

Next was the solar array. Built the frame and wrestled with fitting the panels. Bloody charge controller was shot. So much so the battery cable overheated and became squidgy, the fuse melted and the crocodile clip started smoking...

I'm knackered...

Wednesday 28/07/10

Drove an hour to the nearest Maplin shop to replace the duff controller. Also took the opportunity to do a top up shop at the supermarket. Already pretty settled. Busied myself 'mulching' the willow beds. Basically this involves putting down recycled cardboard to keep the grass down then shovelling cow poo onto it. Good fun, with some music going...

Ayres, the guy we're helping, spent the day creating pathways and building bridges over drainage ditches.

Over the coming days alot of time will be spent preparing the site of the first build ensuring all materials are on hand.

The Diary Of A Warless Warrior

Finally got round to shoring up our caravan door. The wood had come away from the hinge. A couple of nails, hammer, bit of flashing, tin snips and wayhey! Well, for the time being. May very well need to replace a large portion of the door with fresh wood, but time will tell.

Am eager to try out the solar shower, however... no sun... guess a boring old wash will have to do.

Tomorrow I have decided to construct a washing up table out of some pallets, and maybe a bench.

Anything we can do in the awning rather than in the caravan, will help keep people from having to dance around each other.

Thursday 29/07/10

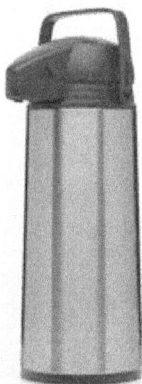

Our Stainless Steel Pump Pot

Used the rocket stove instead of the gas this morning to boil the kettle. Took ages. Mostly down to the dew. Stove needs some tweaking anyway, still, did the job. Chucked the boiled water into a flask - instant caffeine shots. Right! Table time!

My Triumph.

Table was a resounding success. Quite chuffed with my recycling and engineering. Used one pallet, actually less because I was left with some nice kindling.

Next item and project. Shower. Used three lengths of hazel lashed together. Tested it out as well, passed, but needs tweaking. Height. Solar Shower needs to be raised. Covering. Tarp is ok but will probably need another.

Plus positioning is a factor. Am not concerned so much about nudity, but others exposure it...

Friday 30/07/10

Replaced a leg of the shower as one was too long and bent meaning it was nigh on impossible to wrap a tarp around. Hit upon a small idea. Remove the hose of the solar shower. Its about half a metre long and if you bend it, it forms a kink and stops the flow. It also means that to have the nozzle above your head, is to no longer be able to reach the tap...

Sunday 01/08/10

A glorious day for a wedding! Was amazing to see everyone dressed up and not in wellies!

A fantastic service under the oak tree by the mill pond followed by a buffet meal in the marquee. With food out of the way the traditional dancing got under way which I thoroughly enjoyed. Eventually the drumming began and I drank myself to sleep, Fantastic.

Monday 02/08/10

Laundry Day.. Took a trip to the 'local' town 20 odd miles away. Seemed hardly worth it for just one bag of dirty washing, but the café bought coffee helped.

Tuesday 03/08/10

Made a bench today. Similar to the washing up table in its design and construction.

Started the build!

Began by making a 'bunyip' essentially just a tube filled with water secured to two posts. This instrument acts as a spirit level between two points. Ayres cut out squares for the post footings whilst I dug part of the drainage trench.

The building site

Have two more volunteers starting work tomorrow, so looking forward to meeting and greeting.

Have set my alarm to start work nice and early. Am eager to keep the momentum going.

Wednesday 04/08/10

Todays building involved various aspects. Drainage, footings and the poles. Our two American volunteers, Dan and Bree, worked really hard and were most impressive. I finished off the extension of the perimeter drainage ditch and then worked with Bree and Emma digging the footings. Dan broke up the soil with the digging bar, Bree and myself scooped it out onto a sieve where Emma sorted out the rocks from the top soil.

28

The Diary Of A Warless Warrior

Around 12:00 Em & I went off to Crymych for some lunch supplies, which we ate in the poly tunnel. When the sun comes out that thing gets unbearably hot!

After lunch work resumed. Emma stripped the bark off one of the supports, I tamped slate into the footing for foundation, whilst Dan and Bree worked some more on the drainage ditch. Ayres busied himself with various tasks but wasn't at 100% on account of suffering from man flu.

The Diary Of A Warless Warrior

Thursday 05/08/10

Continued yesterdays building tasks in good weather. More tamping of foundations, digging the drainage trenches and pole stripping. Ayres was back to full strength after an early night. Hopefully will be laying the perforated pipe and covering with gravel to form the french drain, but am not sure as we're forecast rain until Sunday...

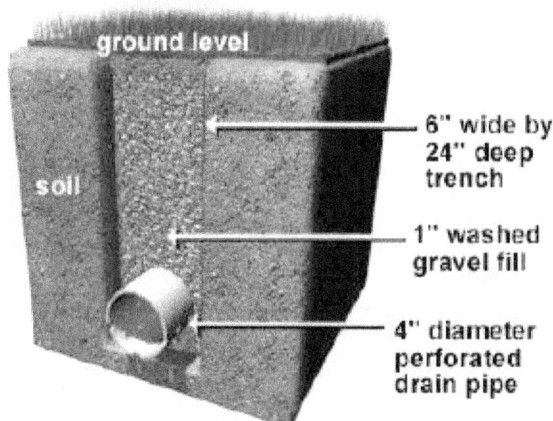

ground level

soil

6" wide by
24" deep
trench

1" washed
gravel fill

4" diameter
perforated
drain pipe

3D art by Marty Hovey

http://www.askthebuilder.com

Friday 06/08/10

Today was spent idling somewhat as rain stopped play. Decided to use the down time constructively and set about digitising my diary through a blog. On site is an agricultural building known as 'the clamp'. Here, residents pay for square footage for storage, but also a broadband connection. The electricity hook up is also used to charge depleted leisure batteries. In here I sat and typed until I felt hungry about 12:30/13:00 . After a quick refuel I then resumed my typing until 17:00 by which time my eyes were squiffy and I'd had enough.

At 20:30 I'd been told there would be a jamming session in the farmhouse so with an armful of firewood I set off. Things didn't really get going until 21:00 and by 22:00 I was ready to hit the hay. I find the rhythms that the group settle into put me into a deeply meditative state.

On my way back I saw Ayres was up and ended up smoking and chatting for an hour on the step outside the caravan. Witnessed a pretty damn impressive shooting star, if that's what it was, but you had to be there...

Saturday 07/08/10

This morning was a late one rising just after 09:00. Plan for the day ; Rubbish, gas, solar panels. Had a bit of a tiff with Emma as I felt her helping the build, then requiring me to help her around the home was diluting our roles and priorities. I am also mindful that if a helpful task such as washing up is done too regularly, it becomes the norm and expected.
I want to remain entirely focussed on what I am here to do.

Loaded up the wagon with empty gas canisters with Ayres, who incidentally was also in the middle of a tiff with his wife...women! Then got the rubbish and recycling on board. Issued with shopping lists, we were ready, just needed next door neighbour, Jude. This meant re jigging the back seat which resulted in a box of dead and decaying slugs falling out of a bag, then sliding down my arm. I brushed off the slime, disposed of the culprits, then joined Ayres at Judes. It was then it hit me. A waft of my arm. The vile stench of dead slug slime... Needless to say a quick scrub up was required. A thorough one too.

Dropped Ayres and Jude off at a farmers/agricultural shop then did my shopping. You can't rush in Wales. Not when there's a wedding on and the cashier is scurrying out of the shop between customers to try and catch a glimpse of the bride exiting the church.

Next stop, Nick the Gas. An Englishman who claimed to be nearly self sufficient bar items such as tea, sugar etc. Amazing bloke, off the cuff I asked if he could knock us up a gas bottle wood burner. His reply "tenner, will have it done by the end of the week". Cheers. We'll see a) if it does get done b) if it costs a tenner. To be fair I'm happy to pay way more than that.

Had a wander with the rifle at sunset. Nothing worth shooting. Did succeed in scaring the crap out of the neighbours who I called on to let them know their rear car window was wide open. In all honesty, to have a camo'd up stranger with a mahoosive rifle rock up to your caravan after sundown in Wales could be unnerving I suppose.

Sunday 08/08/10

Took the rifle and headed out a beautiful, clear and sunny morning. First off, I came across a small rucksack, upon inspection I found a child's change of clothes, a sleeping bag, and a y shaped stick. I think I know what the owner has in mind...

The Diary Of A Warless Warrior

Next discovery was that of a camouflaged caravan nestled almost impossibly amongst the trees.

Was a useful exploration of the surrounding countryside.

The Diary Of A Warless Warrior

The Diary Of A Warless Warrior

Being a Sunday, the day has been pretty slow paced. I wandered over to the building site to break up some of the larger stones in the foundation footings. Not 5 minutes in, I managed to drop the whole weight of the tree stump I was using on my (formerly) big toe. Still haven't finished 'walking it off'.....

Helped out Kit whose wedding we attended with the clean up of the Marquee from 17:00-19:00, but aside from that chilled out.

A rare luxury was our pork joint for dinner, as meat has slipped down the menu and courgettes have taken over.

Monday 09/08/10

A very leisurely start to the day. Up around 09:00, finished breakfast and admin around 11:00. Still quite a novelty. although this will inevitably change when Frances returns to school and we effectively end up back in a weekday 9-5 routine. More tamping and foundation work. The slow start has been tolerated due to the weather. Started out grey and drizzly but at times unleashed some glorious sunshine. Rain returned at 17:15 which was convenient. Perhaps not if I end up going with the guys to play football.

Tuesday 10/08/10

Put in a good solid days work and completed digging out the drainage trench. The layout has now evolved so that the two channels join to a pond. This will not only serve to be an aesthetic garden feature, most likely housing fish, but will also reflect sunlight up into the house in accordance with permaculture principles.

Damn good thinking I say.

The evolution of the pond feature iterates the advantage of not building with architectural drawings and blueprints. The build is allowed to flow with ideas, which can manifest as and when circumstance allows. The end result is invariably unique and all the more beautiful.

The Diary Of A Warless Warrior

These visitors just can't hack the pace.

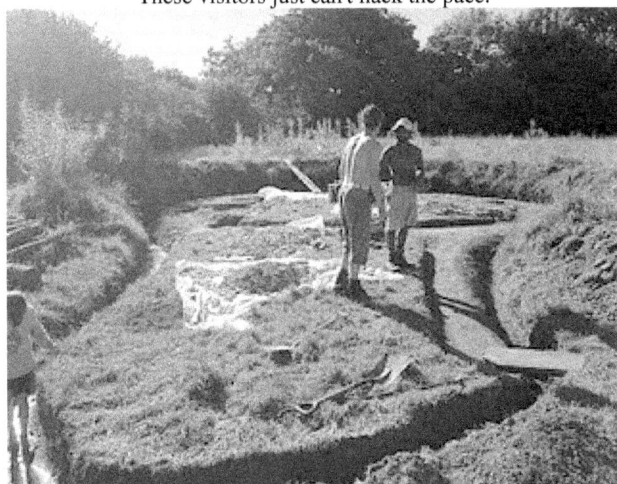

Evening was spent around a washing machine drum fire and very quickly bedtime pounced.

Wednesday 11/08/10

Foundation pad with toe crushing tamper

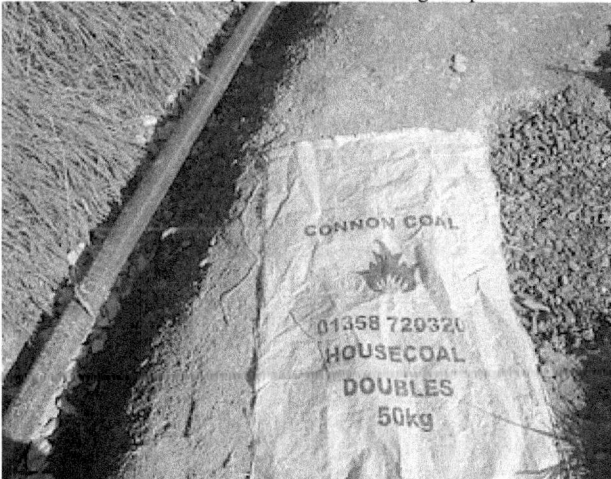

Pipe in trench alongside polypropylene sack that will be used to create a silt barrier.

More tamping of foundation pads and now the perforated pipe has been laid. This is the basis of what is known as a French Drain, Essentially just a rubble trench, as with anything, there are many ways of achieving the same effect. The simplest is a gravel trench the most elaborate being with a pipe sock and eco textile lining.

Thursday 12/08/10

A day off, of sorts. Meeting my parents up in Llandovery to hand over Frances who'll be going on holiday with them to Devon until Sunday next.

Whilst there, will need to run a few errands and visit the laundrette. Evening was spent chatting to Ayres and his in laws. Another Meteor shower meant to be going on...

Friday 13/08/10

When you immerse yourself in a world of green building, it won't be long before you hear mention of reciprocal roofs. Well without experience of building these, I don't know much about them, but by God if I haven't just married that with my favourite commodity.. BEER!

Behold! The worlds first reciprocal fridge!

Saturday 14/08/10

A very pensive Ayres...

Birthday party! Celebrated Ayres' son Ellians birthday with a visit to the beach at Poppit sands. Weather was brilliant if a bit windy. Topped the day off with a rare luxury - Ice Cream! A Magnum Classic. Classic.

The Diary Of A Warless Warrior

Sunday 15/08/10

Absolutely glorious weather. The sort of weather that beckons you to venture out. Emma and I took the opportunity to call upon some other plot holders. First stop was Paul and Hoppi's where Paul was engrossed in the creation of a family board game. This entailed a papier mache mountain range along with streams, meadows and 'forests' of gathered grasses. Was bloody impressed! Would appear to be Pauls calling to create awesome places people enjoy being involved in.

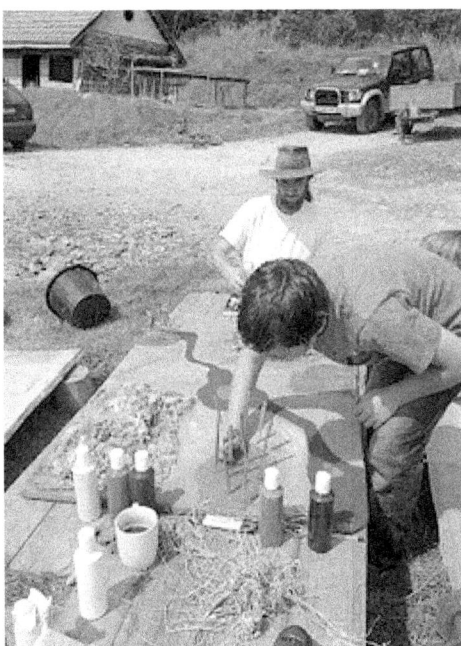

Had a few cups of tea and a good chat with Hoppi (Paul was in his element and far too involved lol) then it was off to talk beer with Kit and Saara. Kit was extremely taken with my idea of a brewing co-operative and 'Man tent'. So we paid a visit to Simon D's whilst Emma and Saara gathered Rowan Berries.
Simon is no stranger to brewing and is in possession of a recipe book of all

sorts of weird and wonderful brews Sacred and Herbal Healing Beers: The Secrets of Ancient Fermentation.
His suggestion was to try using yarrow instead of hops or perhaps meadowsweet. He also allowed me to take one of his brewing kits, a Caxtons Best Bitter and some sugar and go off and start brewing! Yey! The Tir-Y-Gafel Brewers Co-operative has begun*. I'm interested to see how the brew pans out without the aid of my trusted 'Brew Belt'.
Kit invited us over for dinner, a potato curry. Most delicious. Have decided to go to Cardigan with Kit tomorrow to visit the brew shop.

Monday 16/08/10

Set off just after midday with Kit & Saara for a trip to Cardigan. Had a small shopping list from Ayres, but the main aim was to visit the brew shop. Of course it was shut on Mondays... So we filled the afternoon mooching around various shops, mostly charity ones collecting some pretty good bargains. I was particularly pleased with my purchase of two books: Brewing Beers Like Those You Buy and Amateur Winemaker recipes

The trip ended with a supermarket shop and then it was off to grab fish and chips in Crymych before us lads went off to play football in Maenclochog.

Had a good run around that saw us troop down to a seemingly near bankrupt village pub, and after another beer at Kits it was time to welcome the warm embrace of my bed and sweet restful slumber.

Tuesday 17/08/10

Had the morning to ourselves which was spent doing odd jobs and reading. Put in a couple of hours work on the gravel and the drainage trench from 14:00 - 17:30. After a bite of supper we headed over to a field by the community hub (Yurt) where a few of us played 'Ultimate Frisbee' led by the American visitors Dan and Bree. Was absolutely shattered by the time I hit the hay at 22:00.

Slugs share my 'spidey' sense for a good brew!

Wednesday 18/08/10

Another trip to Cardigan, again with Kit & Saara. This time with the wheel of Ayres' daughters bike, a bag of laundry and a visit to the brew shop. Despite having intentions of exploring a mash tun/boiler in order to make my beers from scratch. I have been dissuaded on two accounts by the shop owner. One, the price of hops £5.11 for 500g due to last years floods wiping out the crops in Kent. Two, the price of Barley and malt, now inflated as a result of the Russian crop failure, this time due to drought and water shortages.

After lots more mooching a trip to Tesco's and the reduced section yielded venison steaks!

An evening meal at Kit & Saara's wrapped things up nicely.

Thursday 19/08/10

My Dads birthday today, left a message... Put in some work on the building site which is now simply a case of filling a barrow of sifted stone and dumping it in a trench. We're about 1/4 of the way done.

By 15:00 the misty drizzle came full on with a severe weather warning issued. Despite this Kit and Saara came down for last nights pudding and to watch '300'. Saara was not impressed. By neither the violence nor the man boobs.

A stormy night meant I was up at 04:30 ensuring the awning and the man tent were still secure.

Friday 20/08/10

Drifted back to sleep after an early celestial performance of sheet lightning and far off thunder at 04:30. Was happily eating breakfast when Emma shouted, something about fire in the awning! Nearly broke my leg leaping out of the caravan onto the pallets to find my little 150w car inverter churning out a cloud of smoke (not wholly unexpected baring in mind its intended use). Took the battery to the barn for some topping up and surfed the net checking out inverters, emails, bank balance, then collected everyone's rubbish and recycling to take to the tip on our way to Llanelli and the nearest Maplin store.

Accidentally took the scenic route and on the return leg noticed the car was losing power in much the same way the Galant did the time we broke down at Lammas. This time however I'm pretty certain its the fuel filter after switching to Bio-Diesel. Ideally it needs a full service, but can't afford it right now...

Saturday 21/08/10

Another wet day. Useful in the way I find things that need doing that would otherwise have been forgotten or plain ignored. The slug population appears to have exploded! They get everywhere. Before, I was at ease with their existence. I accepted their presence and unless they were befouling something I held dear we enjoyed a harmonious relationship.

Not any more.

They're in my wellies. They're on the walls, they're on the awning zip ready to ambush you with a film of cold slime. They even hitch lifts in/on the car when you try and escape. Have dreamt up a new pastime and it contains just two ingredients. Slugs, and my nice new air rifle...

Aside from developing an irrational hatred of lower life forms, I also spent some time sorting out my overdue phone bill, watching the great Lee Evans, and typing up my diary onto the blog. My good deed of the day was in the form of helping another volunteer, an Icelandic chap who'd managed to puncture the tyre of his A reg VW camper on a screw. The trouble was, as we used the foot pump, it sank into the ground and sucked up mud, grit and water rendering it useless. I tried anyway...

Sunday 22/08/10

A break in the weather should have meant a window to catch up on some work outside, however Frances is being delivered back today and despite the warm sunshine not much has dried out properly.

My 'eco' washing machine...

To that end much of the day was spent doing very little aside from odd jobs until 15:00 when we were due to meet my parents in the village and guide them in.

Car unloaded, mostly filled with my brewing equipment, YEY! Followed by a coffee, a chat and a guided tour. Unfortunately my parents had to backtrack a fair way to stay at a travel lodge near my sister, so they only had an hour or so with us.

They were very impressed by all that's happening here and hopefully will come again and stay longer.

Monday 23/08/10

Beer recipe research. Am keen to find home brew recipes that don't require ingredients I don't have to hand i.e. malt extract, hops, barley etc. To that end most of the morning and early afternoon was spent on the internet in the 'clamp'.

The only distraction came in the form of two boys who'd found a jar of vintage 2007 sauerkraut and were eager to make a stink bomb using that and a crisp packet...

The only promising lead with recipes came from herbalbeers.com but aside from yarrow, I have no idea where to find mugwort or wormwood. Wormwood has psychotropic qualities so am most excited to hunt that bad boy down!

Am on taxiing duties so off to Whitland to collect Ayres after his business trip.

Was rather intrigued by what he had to say. How he's recently come to realise how in conversation, we all speak half truths. Not that we're dishonest but its also down to the questions we ask and are asked. One of these I personally have always had trouble with is "How are you?" And this is Ayres's point. Relative to what? "How are you?" - Well I'm not dead, so yes I might be considered medically sound. So the answer "I'm well" could be considered truthful...

Ayres's analogy was along the lines of observations or statements such as "It's cold isn't it" You might agree even though you perceive it to be warm. Again this can be measured but the question "Relative to what?" The Arctic? Hawaii? The Sun?!

That conversation has stuck with me and made me think.

I like that.

Tuesday 24/08/10

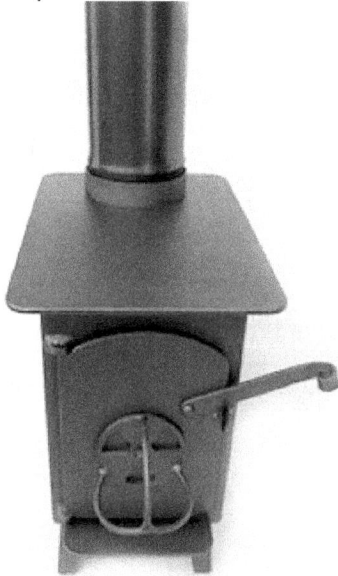

Our new 'Wendy' Wood burning stove

Wood burning stove arrived today just as the family we're helping left for the beach with some friends who are visiting.

Without help or instruction I set about ripping out the gas heater and punching a hole through the caravan wall for the flue. This is in spite of advice to go through the roof. The wisdom of this advice became apparent when I lit a small fire and got a thick stream of smoke billowing into my face. When Ayres returned he was exceedingly concerned with the whole set up which I already knew to be unsatisfactory, but to have a respected friend voice it really left me down about it.
That said, after dropping off Kit and Saara at Clunderwyn station and some fish & chips, I've had a rethink.
Patch up the damage and follow everyones advice. Go through the roof!

Wednesday 25/08/10

A trek to the nearest stove shop, a good 20 miles away. Explained the situation and came away £104 poorer. Bought cowling, flashing, a 'storm collar' and a 4" to 5" adapter. Wet and windy today so will wait for a lull before attempting anything. Sods law this evening has been bloody cold.

Thursday 26/08/10

Got the car booked in to get the fuel filter changed. Picked up a new filter on the way to the stove shop yesterday, so just a case of swapping it over. Attempted it myself but broke a neighbours filter strap in two places, so I heeded the gods warning and paid a professional.

The morning was spent against the clock and the weather, but now we have a properly installed and fully functioning wood burner.

Might need to buy a smaller kettle....

This evening was the opposite to last, was absolutely roasting! A fire truly does turn your shelter into a home.

Friday 27/08/10

Got a trailer load of logs on the way today. Should see us through until Spring. Not bad for £35! Went to get the cash this morning in order to be back to erect a dome. What type of dome, I wasn't told. All I was asked was to report to a certain field at 11:00 in order to help erect a dome for an hour. Went to the field at 11:00, no one there. No Dome. Hung around until 11:20. Not good as logs coming at 12:30. Eventually Paul came by around 13:00 after the logs had been delivered to ask me to go back as Will and Jam had arrived. Had got the kids building a log wall at the back of a tent, I doubt it'll take long before the novelty wears off.

The Diary Of A Warless Warrior

Reported back to the field and worked until 17:45 building a "geo-dome with a Bedouin twist". Basically a dome with marquee canvas thrown over and pegged down. The dome was a '3 frequency' dome with plastic piping melted onto the ends of three different lengths of pole. Short Medium and Long. These were laid out in a specific pattern and then bolted together.

As this was done it pretty much built itself. So impressed am I, I reckon I'll build my own. Far better than a yurt or bender in my opinion.

The finished dome. Four hours after start.

The Diary Of A Warless Warrior

Internal view of the geo dome

Close up of the geo dome joints.

Fran in the geo dome.

Saturday 28/08/10

Great to see people meeting, greeting and sharing.

The Diary Of A Warless Warrior

A day of various activities ranging from tours to 'visioning' and guided meditation, to group work and lectures. All about how Lammas has come to fruition and how it can be replicated and reproduced. For me, its been fascinating to see the wide ranging backgrounds these like minded people are coming from. Some wish to retire to an eco community, others have land, others money, some with nothing but a burning and pressing desire to live off the land. Its a jigsaw puzzle that needs jigging so all the pieces fall into place, however, everyone is waiting for the other to take the leap, to create, so they can join.

Some of the most productive time has actually come from around the camp fire in the evening, where people have networked, explained their particular circumstances, and exchanged contact details and resolving to go further. Time will tell and separate the wheat from the chaff.

Sunday 29/08/10

The round up. I got the time slightly wrong so arrived a tad late. The group was arranged in a circle and giving their views on both the relevance and meaning of the weekend to them, and what they intended to do from now.

I was disappointed. By the group itself. As I said in the circle, it was quite apparent that the various circumstances of the individuals, the resources were all there to set up an eco village. Money, land, me the willing to volunteer etc But it was a jumbled jigsaw. A complete jigsaw that needed sorting. And therein lay the problem, each piece was looking to the other expecting someone to pick them up and put them in their place. This frustrated me no end.

All were unhappy with their current standing, yet none appeared willing to hold up the torch and get creating.

I loved an exercise Hoppi got us all to do. Everyone formed a circle, stood heel to toe with arms through the arms of the person in front and placed on their waist. We all sat down on the count of three. Each supported the weight of the other. Has to be done to be appreciated I think.
Walked up to Simon's and discussed my thoughts with Ayres and Simon, will talk to Paul tomorrow and hopefully get this dream manifested.

The Diary Of A Warless Warrior

Didi, our host family's cat was most satisfied with our Wood Burner...

Very satisfied indeed

Monday 30/08/10

Pounding. Shovelling. Sifting. Dumping. This French drain is taking ages.
Paul came to see me around 17:00 and we had a lengthy chat about my
options with regards to buying land and replicating the Lammas model. All
very encouraging, his pledge to support my efforts, most assuring. I just need
to secure investment of probably £30k-£60k to get the ball rolling. Alot of
money to someone without any! And its that alone that daunts me. All the
rest has been done before. I guess so has the financial side...
Now my time or more specifically my thinking time, is consumed with these
plans and ideas. Something will formulate but I know that even that will take
time.

Tuesday 31/08/10

So far a week of fantastic weather. All good for building. Tinkering with the
foundations of the timber post. The aim is to get them level, which will make
life easier rather than being a necessity. Andy, another plot holder, has gone
the other way and not bothered, electing to cut each timber. Steady progress.

Wednesday 01/09/10

Have exhausted our supply of the black slatey stuff, not too big a deal though, as we're going for a sunrise/sunset theme with the gravel. This means its back to the subsoil pile to sift out more of the light stuff. Along side this, more poles need stripping. Asked Ayres how much this project will cost. Probably a question he doesn't like to ask himself judging by the answer. I agree too. How can you put a price on shelter? What will be a home, albeit short term. What about the price of our labour? For the sake of argument an estimate was put around £2500. My reaction was, wow, that's expensive, but that's coming from someone without any money... If you think of the cost of conventional houses its nothing, Pocket change. You pay that much to solicitors alone. Not to mention tax/stamp duty. Really is food for thought.

Thursday 02/09/10

Dropped Fran off at her new school for her first day. Am happy and excited for her but hate the commitment to a routine albeit a 9-3. Just brings about memories of all we've left behind. After dropping her off and having had a tour of the school, it has left me questioning our aims and plan.

Its been quite apparent, in fact, from the outset, that these guys at Lammas are conventional folk like most others trying to reclaim the independence and freedom of our ancestors but without the sacred knowledge they held. As a result, they're going on instinct.

Whilst my intention is of touring and learning this knowledge, I'm reminded by nearly all the residents here that I have an enviable advantage over them. My youth. But I'm conscious this gift is gradually being revoked everyday. So I feel the need to find a way to buy land now and get cracking...

Frans new school. Outside play area complete with Wendy house!

Friday 03/09/10

10:00 meeting for a day trip! Have been invited to tag along for a visit to Brithdir Mawr for a little talk and demonstration about wood gasification and wood gasifiers. This is a subject I actually know a fair amount about. My ulterior motive was to see the set up and enquire about a few things as it was somewhere we'd considered joining after Lammas. Even more so when we'd heard they were looking for members!

Got to meet the fantastic Mr Tony Wrench, author of the book: Building A Low Impact Roundhouse. A real character and bloody nice bloke.

If it hadn't been for my thoughts the previous day, I would probably have said we'd be most likely to go there and live, however I'm torn. They all seem fantastic people. I suppose it depends on what my parents say and whether they can help me raise the cash on some land.

Saturday 04/09/10

Found myself out working until sundown. Am determined to finish off laying the gravel. Ayres was in Bath attending a funeral so it was just me. Without sounding like a hermit, I do enjoy working alone. Its not that I'm unsociable but with some good music in the headphones and a solid rhythm to your work I find I can really get things done without my mind and endless thoughts getting in my way.

Sunday 05/09/10

Attended what I believe is called a 'Blessing Way'. From what I understand a pagan ceremony where the community comes together to bless the way for a baby to enter this world and come to being. Only caught half of it as the first couple of hours was for the women to get together and do what women do best I imagine. The part us men were invited to involved singing, washing the mother-to-be's feet and offering two beads and a candle. This culminated with a ball of wool being woven around the circle, which was then cut and tied around each individuals wrist. Not to be removed, until mother and baby returned safely back from hospital.

Crap weather forecast, so may continue updating the blog. Have enjoyed reading Katy and Leanders blog. millpondpostcards.wordpress.com . Especially his humorous post about 'Munchman Flap Jacks'.

Monday 06/09/10

Rain. Kind of useful for everyone judging by the busyness of the clamp. There are no days off. Just different jobs that need doing.

Got a call around 13:00 from Ayres to ask for a lift back from Laurence's Garage due to his brake pads wearing out and grinding the discs. Was then time to pick up my truck load of kids, made interesting when Paul drew up exclaiming "Follow me!". Cool. Colin McRae mode, welsh rally stage. Doubt Monsieur McRae ever ran into a Freelander that was incapable of reversing... Was still a cool route which brings the school run into a loop. Have made a mental note to take more photos to liven up the blog. No excuse now digital photos are free. Borrowed 'Earth Sheltered Houses' - Rob Roy, from Simon D

Tuesday 07/09/10

It appears that leading a life independent of the marketplace (kind of) and everyday hustle and bustle comes at the cost of being out of sync with the rest of the busy world. Yet again, we took a trip to Cardigan only to find the banks and most of the shops shut. A bit ridiculous as the time hasn't changed. Now learnt the banks shut at 16:30 not 17:30 so I guess we can be forgiven somewhat. Its something more though.

One noticeable change has been when we pass an estate agents window. No longer are we looking for houses, but rather land. Emma says she now catches herself eyeing up other caravans!

I already find the volume of cars both intimidating and bloody annoying. As well as the fact I have to urinate in a designated place, and not behind a handy bush...just a personal grievance.

Am in the pathetic situation where I've been sent some cheques from my parents, but can't pay them in as my bank doesn't have a branch for miles. So I now have to send them back for my parents to pay in.

Aside from the above, had a chilled out day with the hosts cat on my lap. She just wouldn't move, and because I then couldn't lean forward when eating, she got a nice dusting.

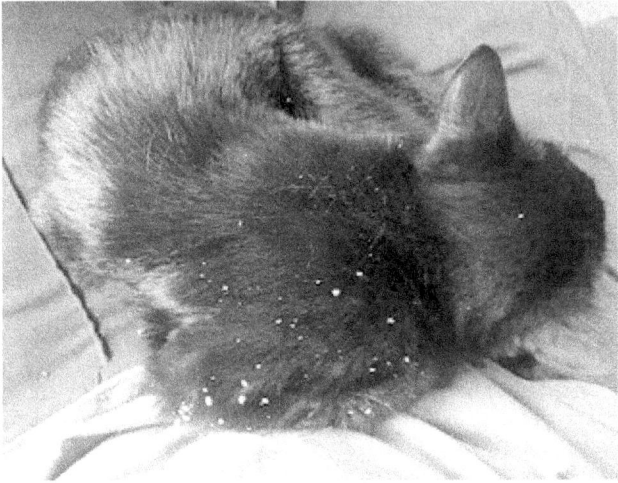

She enjoyed licking herself clean though...

Wednesday 08/09/10

Mist hanging in the valley.

The Diary Of A Warless Warrior

Cool date! No work due to weather. Finished reading Earth-Sheltered Houses which I borrowed from Simon D. Interesting, but the author uses far too many modern materials and cop outs for my liking. The techniques are good though as well as the explanations and illustrations.

Ayres went off to collect his mother from Cardiff. Exciting stuff as she's coming from California!

Have been researching our options and looked more at Tinkers Bubble in Somerset. Seems like a definite possibility. Am mindful of the distance and the fact there are so many communities here in Wales that it would be silly to leave and come back. Would be useful to spend a rainy Saturday/Sunday visiting local places.

Thursday 09/09/10

End of French drain that will hopefully feed a pond

The Diary Of A Warless Warrior

Where dark and light gravel meet to give Sunrise/Sunset effect.

Building site so far.

The Diary Of A Warless Warrior

Was pleased and eager to be outside today. So much so, I was out past 20:00. Worked until I could barely see and a wood chip jumped up and smacked me square in the eyeball. Called it quits after that.

11 hours take the time spent on the school run and taking the children to the language centre.

Parents are invited to learn Welsh too to aid their child's learning. I completely agree, however couldn't help thinking "Yeah, but we won't be here that long..." So either we be here that long and commit to all the various initiatives, or we decide on what the hell we're doing with regards to the next place we're going. If its in England, then perhaps its not a productive use of our time. Although I'm all for not only us, but Frances learning Welsh, we have so many options and therein lies the problem.

Here are the options as I see them;

1) Leave in October for a place like Tinkers Bubble, where we can settle, or at least stay for the foreseeable future.

2) Stay at Lammas for as long as we're able, risking outstaying our welcome.

3) Buy land locally with the help of parents and replicating what Lammas have done. Either on our own or preferably with a group of others,

4) Buy land in England most likely a derelict farmstead and blazing a trail, again like Lammas. This would require substantial fund raising, but anything is possible.

5) Go WWOOFING

There are of course other factors to consider. Option 3 would be good if done close to Frans existing school which she very much enjoys.

There are 14 acres for sale for around £65000 with woodland, however that's a lot to manage on your own. Plus would only support 2 other families max. A very intimate community... The reality is that it would be further away. Slightly negating that option, but leads to yet another. Am so confused am going to talk to Paul tomorrow in the hope he can impart some wisdom from experience to aid my decision.

The Diary Of A Warless Warrior

I guess this has all come about predominantly through an attack of conscience .

Our daughter has no control and is bound to follow us, her parents. I therefore feel honour and duty bound to ensure we still provide her with the best possible life that agrees with all of us. That will take compromise. But one thing I know for sure, the only definite I have is we will NOT return to 9-5's and 'the system' or the 'Matrix' as one guy called it.

Friday 10/09/10

A wet and windy millpond

Wet and windy today. Invented a game using my diary to test Emma's memory. She scared the hell out of me! She would zone in on an activity mentioned or memorable detail, refer to another day or date of fair proximity and count. After roughly ten seconds she'd get the day, not long after that she'd generally get the date too, although her counting would sometimes lead her astray. The incredibly embarrassing thing was that when she tested me I was way out. Not a clue. Even on days I had tested her on ten minutes prior!

I'm the first to admit my short term memory leaves a lot to be desired but boy did that shock me. And I'm only 25 years old. That's without abusing drugs, sure I enjoy my alcoholic beverages, but I'm hardly an ageing rock star!

Imagine what I'll be like when I'm 80 and senile. Will need more than this diary. Will probably have to draw a map just to know where my arse is! Best do that now before I forget....

Saturday 11/09/10

Yum Yums Sweets, Cardigan

Made another trek to Cardigan, rushed to get there before midday to catch the bank. Still too late as this branch obviously felt Monday-Friday were the only days their customers needed to administer their accounts.

Still, made the most of it by grabbing some sweets and an ice cream as well as some supplies from the supermarket. Had a very chilled out, but short evening as we went to bed at 20:45!

Sunday 12/09/10

The growing pile of stripped logs

Where the butchery takes place

The Diary Of A Warless Warrior

The Diary Of A Warless Warrior

The Diary Of A Warless Warrior

In the morning we had a sit down chat with our host family. Was good to look forward and back on our time thus far. So good in fact, we have resolved to make it a monthly thing.

From there I took Frances, Davey and Bee to a birthday party in Llanfyrnach. Then wandered up to Pauls to gain some clarity. Amongst the many things we talked about, the bit of advice he gave that has been most useful right now is the saying "It is better to do nothing, than the wrong thing". To me, that says, chill out, hang tight and allow events and opportunities to unfold and present themselves.

In order to digest all that Paul had kindly imparted, I spent the rest of the afternoon stripping more poles under a surprisingly warm sky.

Ended the day around an open fire chatting to a select group who had gathered to honour another volunteers birthday.

Monday 13/09/10

The Circus?! Lions?Tigers?Bears? Nope - Katy and Leanders Roundhouse

Weather has turned. The next 48 hours are supposed to be high winds and rain. Despite this, I was amazed to see what appeared to be a circus 'Big Top' being assembled over on Katy and Leanders plot! In actual fact this massive red tarp was being spread over their roundhouse to allow them to finish the roofing.

Ayres and I waterproofed up to do some of our own building work, but decided to go and offer a hand whilst having a nose around.

We broke for lunch and I was busying myself cutting kindling, when for the second time so far I heard "Mike! FIRE!"

Fireman Mike was once again employed. This time to quench a pan of oil Emma had succeeded igniting. As I'm sure everyone knows, these can be potentially catastrophic if treated in the wrong way. Knowing that water would unleash a deadly napalm bomb I slid the lid over the pan in the hope of starving it of oxygen. This appeared to work until the lid, which was a size too big slid off. The pan then 'popped' and emitted a fireball and a jet of flame threatening to burn a hanging tea towel and the overhead cupboards.

With the lid carefully secured in place, the pan was taken outside where I was greeted by a train of excited children who had seen the flames and were all hoping to be the first to see our lives in carnage.

Sorry kids, I'm just too good.

I am of the opinion Emma secretly hates our new lifestyle and is progressively attempting different methods to destroy it! Will keep an eye on her I think.

Tuesday 14/09/10

Had an extremely vivid nightmare last night.

I was touring the countryside looking to buy some land, when I came across a dusty derelict farmstead. Next thing I knew we were living there and Emma was complaining of 'disturbances'. Before long she was being physically attacked by an unseen force. I remember being absolutely enraged by this and doing battle with this thing,. Absolute to the death fighting, but the more angry I was, the stronger the force I was fighting became. Realising this, I consciously forced myself to risk calming, and luckily it worked, the threat melting away.

Suspecting another ambush and far from convinced I had defeated it, I sought the advice of Emma's mum to help protect and rid us of this ethereal menace. She asked for the help of the angels and I was dressed in a silver breastplate and armour. Whilst I could see it and felt it strapped on, it wasn't physical and couldn't be seen by others. Call it spiritual armour. I was assured, should the demon strike again, I would remain unharmed.

Life quietened down and I arranged to talk to the estate agent to learn some of the properties history. I was to expect a visit that day. Very shortly after, a woman arrived. We shook hands and she handed me the sales particulars. As I glanced them over my eye was drawn to an interior shot, where in the mirror I saw the cloudy reflection of a female. I started to point this out to the woman as a poor photographers error, when I further noticed a blur of orange in the corner of the photograph. As though in fact the camera had caught the spirit of a lady looking into the mirror, perhaps doing her make up. Reinspecting the image in the mirror, the face was horribly distorted conveying anger and hatred. It was clear this spirit was that of a former

The Diary Of A Warless Warrior

owner who was distressed at our presence.

I handed the particulars back to the woman and began to tell her what I'd seen, but stopped. Her hair was ginger. Orange. Her coat a reddy tartan. It was her... At lightning speed the realisation set in. "You're her". She gave a wry knowing smile. Before I could ask "But how come I can see you?", the penny dropped. My mind told me. I'm dead. "You killed me" was all I could utter and her smile spread as she lifted her hand and revealed how she had done it. Hidden between her fingers, was a small ball headed pin. Dipped in poison, all it needed, was for me to offer the unprotected flesh of my palm and my life was taken...

Reads like a crap Hollywood horror I know, but boy did it scare the hell out of me... not too badly considering I went on to dream I found my former headmistress living in a yurt behind a training hospital and medical research centre in Tipi Valley. Weird

Night time entertainment over, I took the tiddlywinks to school, went to Cardigan AGAIN. This time caught the Bank. Enjoyed an egg roll, cheesy chips and a coffee before returning home.

Posed for a Lammas group photo, still feel weird about that sort of thing, as I'm rather mindful we're just volunteers.

The Diary Of A Warless Warrior

The Singer sewing machine I rescued whilst working on the bins.

Played with the rescued Singer sewing machine, the first time its been used since we've had it. Was pretty fun using all the weird and wonderful attachments, but best left to Emma I think until I can work out how she threaded the damn thing.

Sun suddenly decided to show after a grey day so nearly all of us grabbed the opportunity to step outside. Spent the evening reading my new books that arrived today bought with birthday money.

One is RSPB Pocket Nature Wildlife of Britain . The other is Practical Self Sufficiency .

The Wildlife book I bought because of the fact it has everything from trees to plants to mammals to flies and beetles matched to excellent clear photographs.

The self sufficiency guide, I bought because it actually shows you how to build, make, brew all the stuff other books just say you can do. Really chuffed.

Wednesday 15/09/10

Rammed earth tyres. The agenda for the day. 6 Volunteers arrived last night from Scotland! A 12 hour drive. An amazing mix of stories. South Africans, Hawaiians, English, American, German. Incredible group. As I got chatting, it transpired they came from a community called Culdees I'd read about a couple of nights prior and had been so drawn to, it was a place I thought we could go to after Lammas.

Worked on the site from 10:00 - 13:30 then went back for half an hour until 15:00 as I had to collect the kids and did another hour or so after that. Was pooped by the end.

On a tea break, Simon took the visitors to his place.

Our first completed tyre...

Quite a few more to go!

Not bad progress. Two more courses to go.

Thursday 16/09/10

Had to engage the brain early today as a school run 'system' was changed. a pre breakfast text flurry ensured the tiddlywinks were covered.

More rammed earth tyres with the guys from Culdees.

Weather has been on and off, but for the most part sunny and dry. Am conscious that the sun is now setting around 19:30 and not rising until 06:56. With the days closing in, I am also keeping a weather eye, as inevitably our productive days will diminish.

Although I'm committed to seeing as much of the building done as I can, I'm also aware the travel urge is creeping in. Is it because of the routine I ask myself? Is this an underlying subconscious thing?

The Diary Of A Warless Warrior

How in control of my life and more importantly, my mind, am I?

Friday 17/09/10

Got a call asking if I'd be up for some paid work Monday. Has led me to try and find a way of bringing in some steady cash without the strings of conventional employment.

Unsurprisingly, the viable options appear rather limited. Online paid surveys? Doubt they're 'easy' money. In order to bring in anything acceptable I'd imagine you'd need to sit in front of a machine for 8 hours a day 5 days a week as your eyesight faded and brain liquefied.

Could write a guide perhaps? Do I have the patience or even know anything of use? I like the idea of perhaps writing some short e-books. Cheap. Short. Am not out to make millions, Just enough so our expenses don't completely drain our accounts each month... That said, isn't that what the whole world is trying to do?

Saturday 18/09/10

Attended Fran's School Fête Was a nice little village affair with various simple amusements including a dunk tank!

I managed to become almost obsessed with the "Guess The Weight Of The Pumpkin" so much so, I snuck a photo of the list of guesses and tried to gain the upper hand using the law of averages. This led me to the answer of 15.56811 kg however when I eventually returned to enter my super accurate 'guess' I was devastated to see more guesses. Still, I couldn't back out, so I paid for my guess and hung around until the very end. By which time there were 23 more guesses! One more. I took another clandestine photo and scuttled off with the vain hope my average had only been minutely changed. No such luck. The new average was a massive 4kg over the previous! Damn you Derren Brown. Where are you when I need you!?

It was no longer, indeed was never, about the prize. Simply ensuring that maths was still a constant in my life. If that bloody pumpkin doesn't weigh 19.27023kgs or even better, my earlier guess of 15.56811kgs, I will simply be distraught.

Frans School

The Diary Of A Warless Warrior

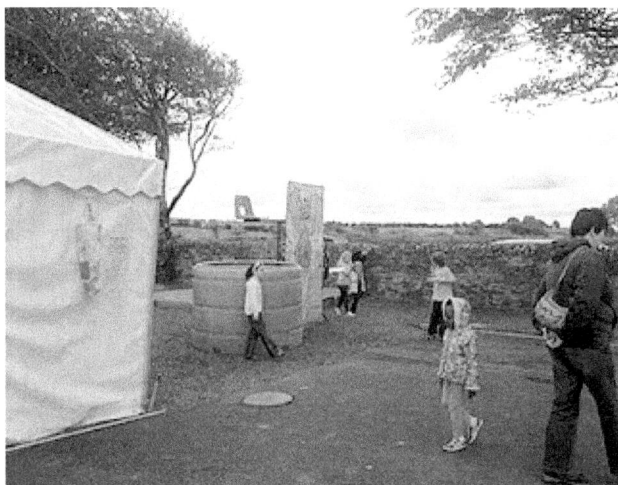

The Dunk Tank, which must have taken ALOT of money that day!

The Diary Of A Warless Warrior

Good old tug of war

Face painting kept Em busy...

Monday 20/09/10

Up early to gather some kit for todays work. Charlie appeared at 08:50 and we set off for Willow's Forest. What greeted me was an incredible 325 acres of Douglas and Norwegian Fir set across a valley.

The Diary Of A Warless Warrior

Our task was to strip the bark off some 200 2m long sections. For this we had a tractor attachment. This machine was basically 2 cogs and a cheese grater. The log was fed in and gripped in a death roll as an alligator might an antelope, then grated at an obscene speed. Was a horrific and fascinating sight. In the first hour it devoured 57 lengths!

Pretty back breaking work and was glad when 17:15 rolled around. 7.5 hours well, 8 hours minus half an hour break.

Got a text to say there was football going on. Was torn. I was pooped, but at the same time liked the sound of a kick around, even if it made tomorrows labour even more painful.

I decided to go as I felt if I didn't on the basis of work the next day, and being tired from todays toil, I'd be living to work and not the other way around.

We left in Ayres' car and were delayed as one of the guys was a volunteer who needed to erect his tent whilst it was still light. On the way we met a large 4x4 coming the other way driven by a woman who looked far from confident at passing in such a narrow lane. Therefore Ayres had to squeeze further in than was necessary. She passed fine, but as we pulled back out BANG! Ayres gouged out a chunk of his front tyre side wall and a large part of the alloy rim. Not good. He dropped us back, understandably rather pissed off and we took my truck. As a result we only played 30-45 mins but that suited me just fine. Feel sorry for Ayres though...

Tuesday 21/09/10

The Diary Of A Warless Warrior

All this machinery means just one man can maintain and harvest this huge forest.

Round two. One man down, so with Charlie and Ritchie on the receiving end I fed the logs through on my own. Right up until 14:30 when the machine broke down. Left at 16:45 making it a 7 hour day. Stopped off at Glandy Cross to pick up some bits after visiting Charlies partner, who, incidentally is working on a farm due to be taken over and run by the owners of Ruskin Mill in Stroud!

Have been offered another day, possibly two of work, but I have turned it down. Partly will welcome the change of pace, plus helping Ayres on the building, is what I'm here to do and this week we have some volunteers to help.

Plus I am fully aware that should I start bringing in money, we'll find things to spend it on. Am currently enjoying not spending by virtue of not having anything to spend!

Wednesday 22/09/10

This week being a volunteer week at Lammas, we have 2 extra pairs of hands. Ayres has been making use of them with a variety of tasks being set. Alot is needing doing. Bales need moving, trees need staking, beds need resurrecting, as well as poles needing stripping (by hand!). With today being the first day of autumn, there was certainly an autumnal feel i.e. the weather was shit. Whilst I agree with the saying "There is no such thing as bad weather, just bad clothing" I still prefer to keep dry. Water proofs are ok, but with hot work they soon lose their benefit as you overheat and become drenched in sweat.

Am becoming concerned about our battery. The controller is now reading between 12 and 11.3 volts. Not sure how to gauge the state of the battery from that, but I guess its low as up until now its rarely dipped below 12 volts. I now have a choice. Spend my earnings on a service on the car, ensuring mobility, or purchase an auxiliary form of electricity generation in the form of a 50w wind turbine.

Being that I <u>could</u> just charge the battery in the barn off mains, I guess logic would dictate I opt for a service. But a service is just so boring...

Thursday 23/09/10

Another pair of volunteers. Put them to work stripping logs but also made full use of having 4 people by using a bearer system to carry poles from a pile at the bottom of the plot. Just as well too as they are predominantly of a larger diameter of Japanese and European larch. After a conversation with one of yesterdays volunteers, Ayres has now decided to extend the building by putting an indoor/outdoor space to the front.

The theory being this would serve to capture and store more natural heat as well as promote natural convection. There was also talk of underfloor heating using the back boiler he has attached to another wood burner.

Will be interesting to see whether this indeed happens and how it would come together.

Another evolution in the plan.

The Diary Of A Warless Warrior

A volunteer from... No prizes for guessing.... that's right, Tipi Valley!

Gappy loses another tooth.

Saturday 25/09/10

Took a walk up the top past Simon D's. A beautiful spot apparently owned by a Belgian couple. Rather selfishly if you ask me. You could fit another Lammas again up there. Plus, it kind of goes against the eco principles being that they've bought 28 acres. The common notion is that roughly 5 acres is enough to support one family. Anything more than that cannot realistically be managed by one household without the employment of mechanical assistance.

Still. We wandered down through the woodland coming across a wonderful variety of wild flowers and wild produce. Mistook an Earthball for a Puffball! Well, only for a split second. After squeezing the top I revealed a chamber of spores and with the help of my new RSPB Wildlife Of Britain book, I learnt the differences and the fact the Earthball is in fact poisonous.

The Diary Of A Warless Warrior

After showering at Ayres' I found myself reading a great little book called Keep Calm and Carry On: Good Advice for Hard Times. The inspiration for which, was the third of three wartime posters, the last of which was never issued. This final poster with this simple message, was to be plastered in tube stations should the Germans have invaded. I love its Britishness.

Tried to watch Yes Man but our charge controller put an end to that with a low battery warning. Had a hunch the shorter days were taking their toll on our solar panels. Had an idea to hook up a bicycle to a washing machine motor and a rectifier. Half to an hour a day on that should provide all of our electrical power...In theory.

The Diary Of A Warless Warrior

Cherries? I hope so as I ate one...

Sunday 26/09/10

Took a stroll around with Em and Fran. Bumped into Paul W and a couple of chaps from The Guardian. Those guys don't seem to be able to get enough of this place. I swear they have done at least two articles already.

Ended up with serious land envy. Seeing all the tracts and imagining what I'd do with it. Ridiculous, I know when you haven't a penny to your name. I guess squatting is the only option.

The Diary Of A Warless Warrior

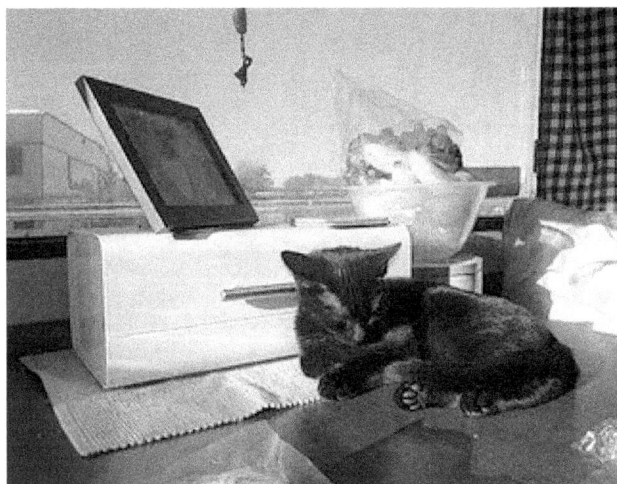

A visit from Didi - or as I prefer to call her Iddy Biddy Diddy Kitty. Her full name.

Tuesday 28/09/10

Simon D had asked me on Sunday whether I was up for some work Tuesday, Wednesday and Thursday. Persuaded Emma to join me. Bit of a mistake. Ended up stripping logs instead of plastering boards with lime - oops. Don't think she'll risk tomorrow.

Had an emotional outburst from Fran last night regarding school. Turns out she's now feeling excluded by the language barrier and being physically and verbally bullied. Ideally she wants to go back to her previous school. Ironically just that morning we'd informed her old school of her new one. Had we not, it would have probably been easy to get her back in, as she was still on the books.

With that in mind, I think it is quite likely we will return at least to England. If only to minimise the impact of this new life on Frans schooling.

The roofing continues.

Wednesday 29/09/10

Lime plaster. But first a punishing session with the gas powered nail gun. My task was to nail thin strips of wood to the panels creating a rough surface for the plaster to adhere to. Punishing, as I failed to notice the heat of the gun burnt the first layers of skin off my thumb!

Next job, plastering. The mix was something like two parts lime 1 part sand? some horse hair in there too... good messy fun to a background of reggae tunes.

Simon D mixing it up

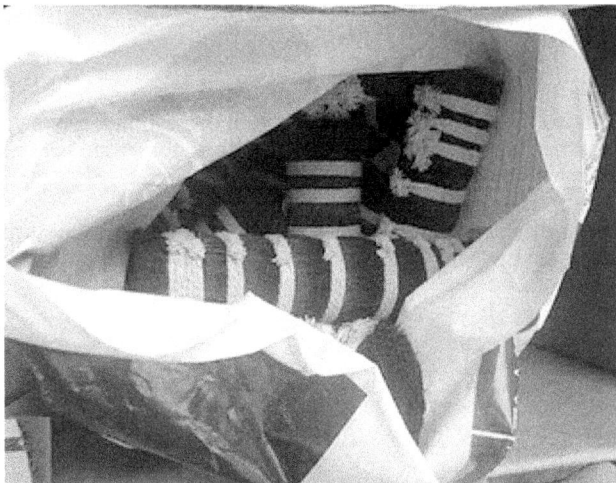

A bag of horse hair

The panels to be plastered.

The Diary Of A Warless Warrior

The 'factory' floor.

Thursday 30/09/10

More plastering, but only two hours today.

Tasted my hawthorn brew today. Definitely alcoholic but rather watery. Noticed the other day the scum that has been sitting on the top had developed a few patches of green mould. Rather hastily grabbed the sieve and scooped that out. Spoke to fellow brewer Simon D about it and to my surprise he told me he'd brewed a damson recipe that had stipulated to wait until such a mould appeared. Don't think I'll leave it much longer before bottling. Am still undecided whether to treat it as a wine and rack it off into demijohns, or add 80g/3oz of sugar for carbonation and bottle like a beer. Am leaning towards wine due to the high alcohol taste and wateriness.

My Eco-Dishwasher being harassed by the cat.

The bales go on Katy and Leanders Roof.

Friday 01/10/10

The battery is dead. The remedy, electrical resurrection. Drove it over to plug it in to the mains. What I didn't take into account was how long it would take to charge a 110 amp hour battery. A 'fast' charge puts in 6 amps an hour, taking 18 hours. Preferable to a normal charge that would only put in 2 amps and therefore take 55 hours! A pain as it means not only relying solely on our two cheap hurricane lanterns, but also Fran will have to go without her usual 'movie night' tonight.

Rang the mechanic, Lawrence, to book the car in for a service. Due to the fact I haven't a clue when it was last done, everything needs doing. The minimum damage - £400! Have arranged to drop it to him Tuesday morning. The justification in my mind is a) this should lower the risk of breaking down in the middle of nowhere b) once done, most areas won't need replacing for two years or so, I hope.

Our celestial power station just ain't juicing the panels like it did...

Saturday 02/10/10

Picked up the battery after its 18 hours of resurrection. Forgot today was a 'Community Engagement' day. The intention of this was to invite the locals to see the progress and answer their questions. A bit difficult when apparently hardly any of the large number of visitors were local. Didn't particularly want to stick around with all the people about so we took a day trip to Cardigan instead.
Whilst there I picked up six of those LED stick on lights, a huge adjustable spanner, 3 books for Frances (Classic Ghost Stories,Children's Encyclopedia and British Wildlife) and some food. Wanted Fish and Chips but they were shut
With the battery back online we settled down to watch one of Frans new films 'The Ant Bully' Pretty entertaining, certainly passed the time.

Sunday 03/10/10

Finally bottled the Hawthorn Brew. Double checked it had finally finished fermenting with the hydrometer. This also gave me the ABV. (OG - FG) x 7.46 + .5 = SG in this instance (1026 - 1000) x 7.46 + .5 = 3.98% ABV.

Gave away four bottles. Two to Katy and Leander and two to Ayres. Barrelled the rest. From the small amount I sampled, what started as a mash that resembled, and smelt like vomit, it appears to have transformed into a pleasant hedgerow tonic.

Monday 04/10/10

Joined Ayres, Simon (the tree surgeon) and volunteer for the week, Helen, in the woods to collect firewood felled a while ago. Had an interesting time trying to turn a land rover and large trailer around on a narrow woodland trail, overlooking a deadly drop...

Football night. This time Ayres joined us. He likened the new pace of the indoor game to watching a Japanese game show. "Blah blah blah Brother. Blah blah blah October". I know what he means. With the ball bouncing around you can find yourself a spectator, but for a frantic few seconds pitched headlong into the thick of the action.

He won't be returning until April when the guys play outdoors again.

I on the other hand have been asked to play in the 5 a side league...

View through the trees.

The building pad being reclaimed by nature after a spell of inactivity.

Tuesday 05/10/10

Paul W invited me up to his for a quick chat. Turns out he wanted to give me the heads up on a really good opportunity to buy some land nearby. We walked over to check it out and it is gorgeous.

We were so taken by it we rang both our families to see if they could help us out. They said no. Couldn't help but feel disappointed. Especially as it is likely to be snapped up by the end of the week.

I guess we'll have to do it on our own, which I respect. I don't want debt, and up until recently, people saved, not borrowed. Since the financial meltdown, it would appear to be our only option. That and wait until the very people we wish to share our experience with, our parents, croak. An unhappy and morbid thought.

The Diary Of A Warless Warrior

Emma using the time honoured method of
swinging your arms to survey a potential building site.

Thursday 07/10/10

Was pre-warned yesterday to set my alarm in order to get up and be ready for work at the ungodly hour of 09:00. This was a shock to the system, as we have gotten used to sleeping our fill each night and rising when we feel we're ready. This is normally around 09:00 and breakfasted by 10:00. Between the numerous and repeated groans and protests from Emma, I joked about how awful a life it would be if you had to do this everyday. The hardship of only being allowed to wake when you feel like it, just two days of the week. Then it hit me. As perverse as it sounds, I believe alot of truth was said in my jests. No other creature on earth forces itself to wake at a set time each day. No other animal in nature forces itself to work when ill. In fact, I dare say, there are very few other beings that continually force themselves to engage in an activity they do not want to do 5 out of 7 days a week, then kid themselves they are happy doing it and that's "just life".

Today was about milling timber. Ayres had booked Adrian and his 'Wood-Mizer' and we processed 13 or so logs. What surprised me was how little usable timber is milled from one tree.

Got a good amount of practice reversing with a trailer which is invaluable when you own a caravan.

By 17:30 I was very tired. Slept soundly in the knowledge no alarm waited to disturb my restful slumber.

The Diary Of A Warless Warrior

Wednesday 13/10/10

Have returned to see friends and family for a week. The whole trip was nearly scrapped after Didi, our friendly neighbourhood kitten, staged a 'sit on' protest.

So far we've crammed in the TV, DVD's and internet but are sorely missing the countryside.
Appreciated, I'm on holiday so to speak, but I have an overwhelming feeling of not being able to do anything. A very painful memory. When you're living in a Barratt box modern home with bugger all land, what can you do? No, or very little garden is great for people who are at work all day busy paying bills.

Night time has literally illuminated something I sorely miss and will prevent me ever returning to live in or near a major city or town.

I miss the stars.

Caught a shot of carpets going over the bales before we left.

Thursday 19/10/10

The Diary Of A Warless Warrior

The Diary Of A Warless Warrior

The Diary Of A Warless Warrior

The Diary Of A Warless Warrior

Arrived back at Lammas at 20:00 Sunday evening. Was a fantastic feeling. Definitely one of returning home, which says alot to me.

Monday morning I was thrown straight back into the mix for what turned out to be a phenomenal days work. It was the stage I have been looking forward to. A stage that gives this build the visual and psychological leap forward into tangibility and manifestation.

The timber framework at this point resembles a henge.

Had great fun playing with a tripod I made with Rudolph.

Although we were only gone from Lammas a week, there appears to have been an explosion of progress and activity in our absence. Andy and Jane's turf roof is on, as is Katy and Leander's, Paul and Hoppi have also finished roofing and waterproofing their barn. And as of Monday morning Simon D has begun work on his workshop and already made substantial headway.

Another leap has come in the form of long term volunteers. We now have 6 more people here, three of whom arrived during the week we were away.

This, and the aforementioned changes have resulted in me feeling rather out

The Diary Of A Warless Warrior

of touch, if not left behind somewhat. Am hoping in a couple of days I'll have settled back in and caught up.

Ayres and Marianne had a visit from the BBC today. Was rather surreal really.

Woke up around 08:30/09:00 and stepped outside looking nicely dishevelled, to be greeted by a camera and sound crew filming Ayres chopping firewood. As sods law would have it, our awning door was right behind Ayres and bang in the middle of their shot. Will no doubt make an entertaining out-take!

We looked after the children whilst the crew interviewed Ayres and Marianne, I think on the subject of money and their relationship to it.

Don't think I can imagine a more mundane 15 minutes of fame quite frankly.

If they had asked me about my relationship to money, I'd have to say it is very much akin to a one night stand, as illustrated by my trip to the petrol station today. Can't help feeling like I've been screwed.

Late afternoon I took to wandering and delivering bottles of my hawthorn brew. Am very glad I did. Was humbled and grateful to meet a chap called Dave, who it transpired was a reader of my blog and gave some very kind feedback. A very very big thank you Dave! Hope to see you back here again soon!

Wednesday 20/10/10

The Diary Of A Warless Warrior

The Diary Of A Warless Warrior

Awake all night pretty much. Enjoyed chatting to Rob, a newcomer who's volunteering with Andy and Jane. We talked until just gone 23:00 sitting inside his rather spacious yurt. Considering it is him on his own in there, it is by comparison to most, positively palatial. Just as I finally clambered over Emma into bed and settled, the heavens machine gunned the roof of our caravan with hailstones. This continued sporadically over the course of the night, the volleys coming in varying degrees of severity.

At 04:00 Fran awoke from a nightmare and complained of cold. With only a handful of kindling to revive the burner, I dressed, and filled a bucket with kindling and logs. This took me a pleasantly meditative half an hour, after which I made us all a hot chocolate.

Another attempt to sleep was sabotaged by my over active and now awake brain and conscience. I was filled with worry and concern for another volunteer, Alexandra. For what must be a month now, she has battled an ongoing saga of trying to get a wood burner in her otherwise heatless caravan. Actually, that isn't entirely accurate. She has a gas heater. That leaks. So I suppose she has the option to fall asleep cosy and warm, never to awake. Anxious to ensure this is resolved ASAP for the sake of her health and general well being. I text volunteer coordinator, Hoppi, my concerns at 05:54. To my amazement, she text back almost immediately! We ended up having a really productive dawn meeting ensuring agreements are amended to prevent the situation arising in the future, as well as putting a plan in place to sort this situation as quickly as possible.

Breakfast, then que my next walkabout. Checked in with Katy and Leander, very impressed by both their progress and ingenuity. For vents to insert through their stonewalling; plastic tubing and mesh cannibalised from a sieve. For roof drainage; plastic pipe, pond liner, inserted with marker pen tops shoved down to secure the liner in place. Further more, it is visibly apparent that the roof drainage is effective and fit for purpose. Well done Katy for that burst of inspiration!
From Katy and Leanders I meandered up to Kits plot where I was promptly press ganged into sorting a pile of bricks into grades and stacking them onto pallets. That took me up to lunch time.

14:30 reconvened with Hoppi and joined by Andy. Have offered myself and Emma to be named contacts should other long term volunteers need any help and support. This I hope, along with monthly meetings, serve to nip any issues in the bud, before they have a chance to blossom into full blown problems. Spent the rest of this very very cold day on idle setting. Am rather exhausted to say the least.

Friday 22/10/10

The Diary Of A Warless Warrior

The Diary Of A Warless Warrior

I believe the day started with a breakfast bowl containing the last of the Weetos purchased during our visit to Stroud. This was followed some time later by the departure of our host family as they themselves visit the town in which they previously resided for the next seven days.

Up until 15:55 I was employed in the service of Kit. My duties included preparation for the digging of the foundations of his build, transportation of timber out of the barn and up to his plot, and very much later, assisting with the marking of the proposed trenches set to be dug at 10:00 Friday morning.

Before his departure Ayres had requested I attend an auction of tools, set to take place in the barn at 16:00, in his stead. The tool he had his eye on and wished for me to bid on in his place, was a fine looking Adze.

Quite what this tool is intended for, I do not at this moment in time know, but Simon obviously did and outbid me. The irony is, Ayres will inevitably end up borrowing it! Over the course of the next hour and a half I got embroiled in numerous bidding wars and came away substantially poorer and the owner of various tools I do not yet have a need for. Delivered a keg of home brewed bitter to Melissa in lieu of her birthday party on Saturday, then it was up to Kits plot to mark his building pad by the light of my trucks headlights.

Another restless night which forced me to Ayres' static caravan for some midnight green building research.

Friday morning I met Kit on his plot at the arranged time of 09:30. A few cigarettes and two coffees later the excavator arrived. Not at 10:00 but more like 11:00. Once we got started and stuck in, we worked hard until we broke for lunch at 13:00. Justin, a volunteer on Nigel's plot and yesterdays auctioneer, borrowed my truck to tow a trailer to carry sand. Due to odd jobs springing up, they had not finished with it at 15:00 as agreed. This made me late leaving for Cardigan and cost me brownie points with my dear Lady Love.

Film night tonight. 'A Series Of Unfortunate Events', then bed. God Bless it.

Saturday 23/10/10

Rubble trench laid with reclaimed bricks.

The Diary Of A Warless Warrior

The Diary Of A Warless Warrior

I am officially declaring last night as the last sleeping starkas night for this year. Why? Because its been bloody cold recently, and despite being a 'hot' sleeper I've managed to contract a phlegmy cough and a runny nose. From this day or rather night, forth I shall include donning a t-shirt in my bedtime routine. Another reason for mentioning this, is not only is it useful to note, but I would hate to think there were men out there, naked and shivering each night because no one had taken the time to tell them it is now too cold. There. Conscience cleansed.

Took a stroll up to Kits at 13:00 to find him in the dark, reading a book and suffering from a monster hangover. Left him to it. On my return, I observed that wonderful sight synonymous with country living and often pictured in school history textbooks. A human chain unloading 200 odd bales of straw. My feeble excuse of merely observing and recording failed to hold water and I was swiftly press ganged into the ranks.

But around here, if we work hard, we play hard. So at 16:00 the gathering to celebrate Melissa's 40th Birthday began to muster, and around 23:00 an exhausted and beer filled me, made and devoured an egg sandwich, and gladly clambered into his bed. Leaving on his shirt.

Thursday 28/10/10

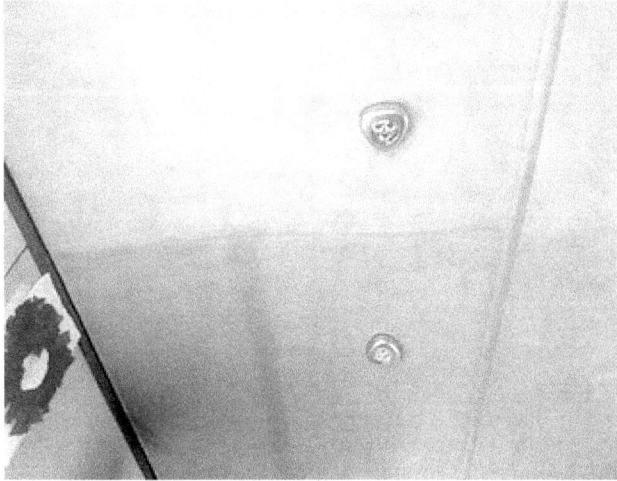

Foolishly, I made a hand print in the grime from the paraffin lanterns, and was made to clean it.
So being immature, I only cleaned my side...

The Diary Of A Warless Warrior

Emma using our rescued hand powered Singer sewing machine for the first time. The cold called for some heavy curtains that made a huge difference.

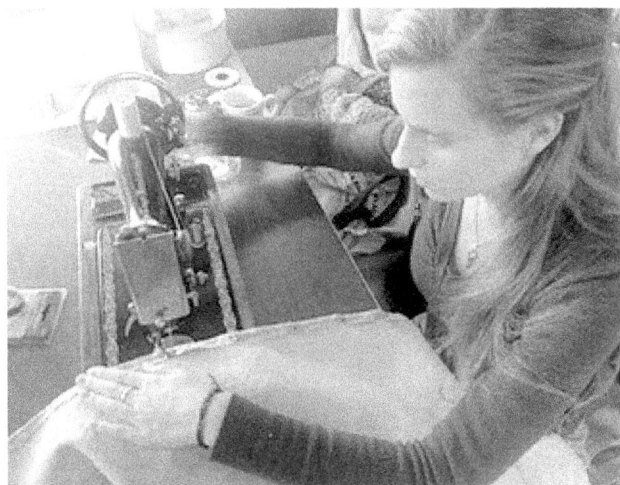

The Diary Of A Warless Warrior

Kit having a quick whack by himself.

Ironically, since Ayres and family departed last week I have been the busiest I've probably been since my arrival. Finished Kits foundations yesterday after a full days graft. He'll now be leaving the rammed stone to wash and settle naturally over the coming week. Well timed too as Ayres returned around 16:00 yesterday.

Monday nights football was very productive, had a fantastic game following which it transpired the oppositions goalkeeper was none other than the owner of the farm next door. This prompted me to suggest us volunteers trooping down to his to help out. This I feel, will give us the husbandry and livestock experience currently lacking at this phase of Lammas' development. Would also help with public relations. Nice and neighbourly and all that.

Tonight we have a gathering of volunteers down at the local pub. I believe its intention is to be a relaxed, informal affair where we can raise and discuss topics of varying importance. Might turn out that the term 'piss up' becomes more accurate...

Saturday 30/10/10

Simon D's latest creation, a workshop.

The Diary Of A Warless Warrior

Kits walled garden. A bit waterlogged.

The Diary Of A Warless Warrior

With an influx of volunteers, this place became quite a work camp. Ayres and I concentrated on building and seating the first cross beam of the henge. Took all day to cut and fine tune two joints. Others were employed looking after the many children, digging a foundation trench for a shed and transporting top soil into raised beds where garlic will be grown.

After lunch a large ominous cloud rolled in and pelted us with rain and hail. In the poly tunnel the sound was magnified making conversation nigh on impossible. Have found myself feeling lethargic and drained. I still haven't shaken my cough. Have resolved to take it easy tomorrow in order to knock this on the head.

Thursday 04/11/10

The Diary Of A Warless Warrior

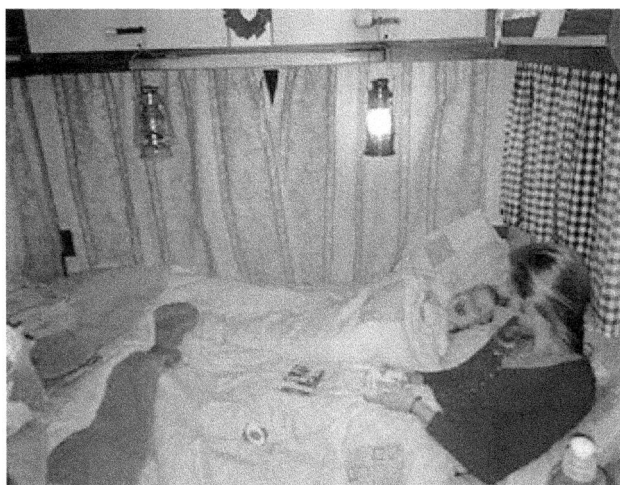

Home Sweet Home

The Diary Of A Warless Warrior

Since Saturday, I've been engaged in quite an assortment of tasks and activities. Helped cut and raise another cross beam on the henge. Its becoming clear that by the way we're doing it we'll be averaging one a day.

Tuesday saw us take a trip to Llanmadoc on the Gower peninsula outside Swansea. Whilst Kit and I packed his things into our truck and his trailer, Em and Fran picked apples and went for a walk. Despite the poor weather and overcast sky some of the scenes around there are most impressive.

We didn't arrive back until late so it wasn't until Wednesday morning that I noticed another cross member had been cut and raised in my absence.

Booked the car in to have a sidelight replaced, as well as have the electrics looked at after the batteries died last Monday night at football. So at 15:00 Wednesday afternoon, kit and I trundled off to Bwlchygroes. We didn't leave there until 16:55 and I'd been told I needed two new batteries. By 17:30 my meagre savings had been wiped out and I was £125.04 poorer. But the proud owner of two Numax Premium Silver 68ah batteries. Forgetting the £80 to fill the tank each time, this car has now cost me in excess of £750 in maintenance this year. A stark reminder of how big a liability these machines are. I could comfort myself in the thought that at least the batteries should be good for the next 5 years, but I liked having savings.

Friday 05/11/10

"Remember, remember the fifth of November, gunpowder, treason and plot. I see no reason, why gunpowder treason, should ever be forgot..."

I'm sure there is some deep meaning and parallel between the events of 1605 and what we are doing here today.

If one looks past the 36 barrels of gunpowder and what would be termed today simply as terrorism, one could possibly recognise both of us are hoping our actions will result in a radical change in society and current accepted methods and beliefs.

But for tonight, Guy Fawkes will return and the inner pyromaniac in all of us that he represents, will rejoice in burning and blowing shit up.

Monday 08/11/10

A game changing day. Emma had been feeling 'off' for the past few days. Being past her sell by date and having inclinations towards incubation, we took a trip to Crymych at 09:00 to get a pregnancy test.

The result was "Pregnant 3+"

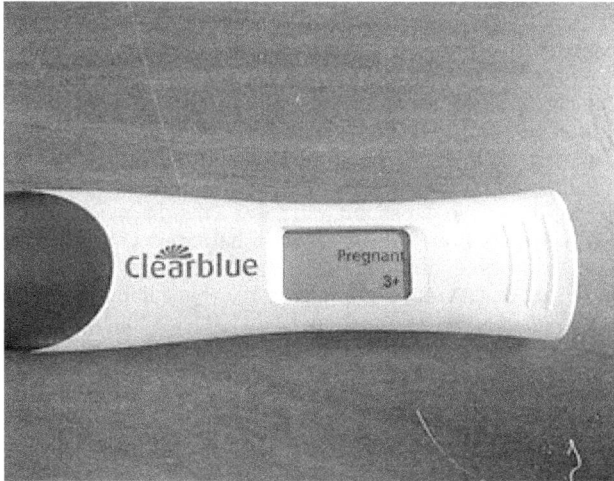

A flurry of text messaging to random folk and an emergency meeting with Ayres and Marianne. Frances took it upon herself to spill the beans before we had a chance, and subsequently faced Emma's wrath.

A serious talk about the whole thing brought forth many ideas and potential possibilities, the main one being to consult Paul and Hoppi. Paul knows the ins and outs of both the planning and the leasehold agreements. therefore is it even feasible for Lammas to absorb another family? It was only designed and got permission for nine. We are looking for long term stability along the lines of 2-5 years. This being the case, I simply don't feel Lammas is the place. We do have an offer from another plot holder that would grants us that, but to accept this would fly in the face of rules and policies. As always one can manipulate such things but its definitely not a practice I wish to engage in.

The Diary Of A Warless Warrior

Here's the truth. We have no right to be here. To remain beyond Spring would tread on toes and upset people we've come to hold dear, and whose generosity has known no bounds thus far. Once more I am writing lists of options and at this moment in time, here they are;

1) Remain in or near Lammas. kits plot verbally guaranteed for two years. Possibility of more living space in the form of a static caravan. Other options and possibilities could evolve from this, but mindful of aforementioned factors.

2) Tipi Valley. Plenty of experience in residents re. Home births. Poor access to lower valley - emergencies. Ideally a Yurt to live in. Would entail logistics moving our life and home. Would be guaranteed for as many years as we'd require. We have visited and know people there.

3) Join a different community. Tinkers Bubble? Would be an unknown unless we used the time we have to make prior visits.

4) Go back home. Ideally rent/buy/get permission to reside on land in a caravan or yurt. Alot of unknowns.

5) Sell out and return to the system be it in Wales or back in Stroud. For me, the least desirable of all. Benefits could be seen as wide and numerous, but at a vast cost spiritually, morally and financially.

6) Squat on land. Extremely unstable. Many variables and unknowns. One important disadvantage, we'd be on our own...

7) Buy our own land. a big ask financially. would require major help from family. Unlikely in probability and unlikely to be finalised in time frame.

8) Wait and see...

Listing is useful. But inconclusive. Will follow option 8 for now. I feel immense pressure to properly lead this family, and lead it well. Its bewildering and overwhelming now. One realisation is that, at this point, nothing has changed. The considerations, yes. But as those who've read previously will know, the options haven't really changed. I've created a mental pressure that has left my stomach knotted and mind exhausted.

If anything, this news has become a catalyst.

The Diary Of A Warless Warrior

Will have to ransom this grandchild if money is the answer.

Hopefully a good hour of football tonight will help clear this over active brain.

Barley shoots growing from a bale weighting our awning down.